I0191593

Chemistry
on the Farm

Mountain Word Academy

from the Mount St Helens Creation Center

Chemistry

Paul F Taylor, BSc MEd

Chemistry: Chemistry on the Farm

Published by:
J6D Publications
PO Box 629
Castle Rock, WA 98611
USA

www.justsixdays.com
www.mshcreationcenter.org
mwacademy.mshcreationcenter.org

ISBN: 978-1-7337363-2-9

J6D Publications is an official publications imprint, through Kindle Direct Publishing - a division of Amazon; kdp.amazon.com

Contents

1. Agriculture in the Bible

There is a great deal that we could say about agriculture in the Bible. Many of the characters mentioned in the Bible were living in a rural setting, where the keeping of livestock or the growing of crops was an essential part of the economy. In this introductory section, it will not be possible to include everything, so we

Adobe Stock Images, licensed to author

will concentrate on some brief notes on the Cultural Mandate, growing crops, and keeping livestock.

The Cultural Mandate

God's Commission to Adam and Eve, in Genesis 1:28 is often called the Cultural Mandate. This is because it can be applied to pretty much any aspect of human activity or culture. It clearly, therefore, has direct application to agriculture.

> And God blessed them. And God said to them, "Be fruitful and multiply and fill the earth and subdue it, and have dominion over the fish of the sea and over the birds of the heavens and over every living thing that moves on the earth." (Genesis 1:28)

Ruth in Boaz's Field, by Julius Schnorr von Carolsfeld (1794-1872), Public Domain image.

After the Flood, God permitted the eating of meat, so the dominion that human beings have over all creatures, and the responsibility to care, or subdue, the Earth, now includes the care of agricultural animals; both as working animals and as food. This mandate requires humans to manage the land, plants, and animals. There is nothing wrong with areas of the world being "unspoiled wilderness", but nor is there anything especially noble about such areas, compared with areas of rural industry, such as farming.

Growing Crops

Adam was set to working the Garden in Genesis 2, though whether this amounts to agriculture, we do not know. But certainly his son Cain was involved in growing crops. We should note that Cain's sins were anger, jealousy, and murder. Not only was there nothing wrong with him growing crops, it is considered a noble livelihood in Scripture.

A brief overview of the importance of food crops can be seen by reading the book of Ruth. It was the failure of the people of Israel to follow God, and to acknowledge Him as King that led to the famine described in Ruth 1. Moreover, Elimelech and Naomi lived in Bethlehem, which means *House of Bread!* There was famine in the House of Bread! And Elimelech's name underscores the reason for this – his name means "My God is King". If only that had been true for the people, there would have been no famine in the land flowing with milk and honey, in the House of Bread.

Later, when the widowed Naomi returns, bringing her young widowed daughter-in-law Ruth with her, Ruth is able to glean grain from the edges of Boaz's field, when the harvest was being gathered, because that was a law permitted to the poor. God's law looked after the feeding of the poor, with His agricultural rules.

Keeping Livestock

You might think that keeping animals on farms would be something that would only happen after the Flood, when we were allowed to eat meat. But animals would have been kept and bred before this. Abel kept flocks, but we must assume they were not for meat. It is more likely that they were for making sacrifices and making clothes – and there would have been a close link between those two properties, given that God gave Adam and Eve clothes of skin to cover their nakedness and shame.

Flock of goats in the Middle East, Adobe Stock Images, licensed to author.

Later in the Bible, animals were kept for sacrifices, but also for food. The Mosaic Law gives provisions for how the animals are to be kept and killed, and while we do not use the same methods of slaughter today, Mosaic rules were in place as the most hygienic available at the time.

Further Study

Research one aspect of farming in the Bible, and write a mini essay (about 100-200 words) about it. If you are working in groups, try to research different passages, so that a broad range of passages in both Old and New Testaments are covered.

2. Requirements for Plant Growth

Field of wheat, CC BY-SA 3.0 Unported

Raising crops requires a detailed understanding of the particular plants that are being grown, and the part of the plant, which is the most use to you. For example, if we are growing corn, then we need to know what chemicals should be provided by the soil, and what conditions are required for growth, especially the growth of the ears of the corn, which are the parts that we will use for food. On the other hand, if we have planted beets, the part of the plant we will use will be the bulbous root. Many of these crops will have been selectively bred for generations and centuries, to enhance the properties of the part of the plant we are interested in. There are, however, some comments we can make about plants in general.

What Do Plants Need for Growth?

Three main elements will be involved in plants in large amounts. These will be carbon, hydrogen, and oxygen. The latter two will be found in water, as well as oxygen gas from the air. Carbon will enter the plants mostly in the form of carbon dioxide, absorbed during photosynthesis, in order to build sugars and cellulose that form the structures of the plants.

There are also a number of other significant elements, usually absorbed through the roots, in the form of ions. The most important three of these are:

- Nitrogen (N)

- Phosphorus (P)

- Potassium (K)

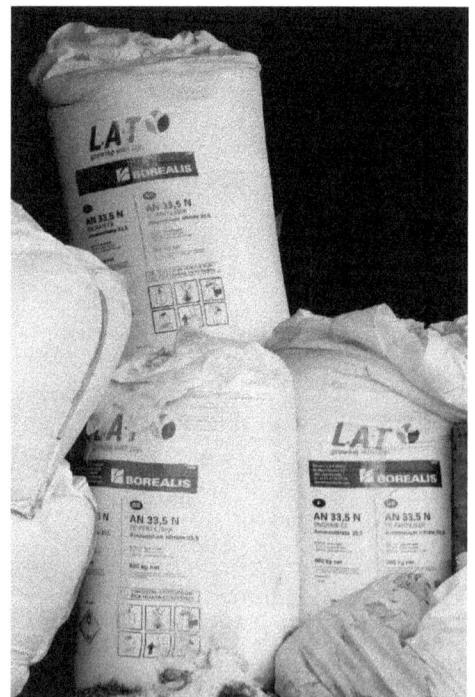
CC BY-SA 4.0 International

Crops will need these three primary macro-nutrients, and local soils may be deficient in one of more of them, so fertilizers may be used to improve plant growth, and these fertilizers may have NPK numbers. NPK numbers are the percentage effective concentrations of the three elements: N is representative of the percentage of elemental nitrogen, whereas the P number is the percentage not actually of the element phosphorus, but the compound phosphorus pentoxide (P_2O_5), and the K number is the percentage of potash (K_2O). Despite the N number representing elemental nitrogen, it will not be absorbed as an element; it will be absorbed either as nitrate (NO_3^-) or as ammonium (NH_4^+).

Although the three elements represented in the NPK numbers are the primary macro-nutrients, there are then three secondary macro-nutrients to consider - calcium (Ca), magnesium (Mg), and sulfur (S). Then there are a number of micro-nutrients – including copper (Cu), iron (Fe), manganese (Mn), molybdenum (Mo), zinc (Zn), and boron (B). All of these minerals (primary and secondary macro-nutrients and micro-nutrients), are absorbed from the soil, in the form of compounds, through the root hairs.

Root Hairs Absorb Water and Nutrients from the Soil

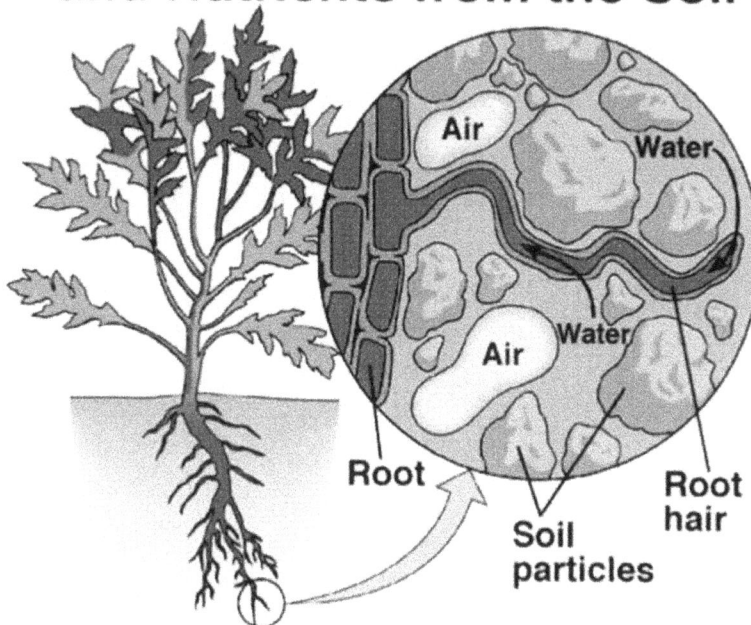

© Aplustopper.com

Fertilizers can be used to alter the relative amounts of these minerals, and to include minerals that are not present. But, in order to use fertilizers, one must know the chemistry of the soil itself, and one must also know the consequences to the local environment of adding too much of a mineral. Some fertilizers may be "natural", some "artificial", but sometimes it is hard to draw the line. It is also worth knowing the other strategies used for soil care through the ages, and the chemical consequences of each.

Further Study

Research the optimal soil requirements for two different food crops. Report on one food crop that you think would grow well in your locale - there may be more than one, so just pick one.

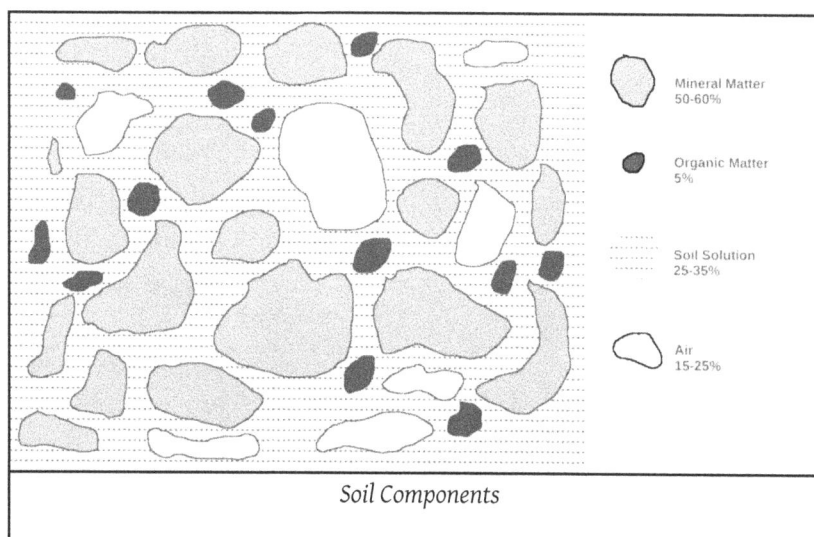

Mineral Matter 50-60%

Organic Matter 5%

Soil Solution 25-35%

Air 15-25%

Soil Components

3. Soil

Typical Soil Appearance

So what actually is soil? It is the material usually found at the top of the Earth's crust, and it is a particulate mixture of small fragments of rock, with organic matter. The mixture works well together, holding both air and water, though we instinctively know that some soils are better than others for different crops. Rock fragments have been produced by the weathering of rocks – by rain, ice damage, "onion skin" weathering, caused by temperature changes, and many others. Clay particles are particularly important, as essential positive ions can bind to their surfaces, and therefore held in the soil.

Weathering

Weathering is caused by a number of factors. Wind can loosen and transport pieces of rock, as can running water. Rain can get into cracks in rocks. If the water freezes in winter, then the ice will expand and cause the crack to grow. After thawing, the crack will be bigger, and the next freezing will open it further. This also causes pieces of rocks to be removed.

Materials expand in warm weather, and rock is no exception. But rock is a poor conductor of heat, so on a hot day, the outside of a rock expands, while the inside remains cold and does not expand as much. This creates tension forces, and the outside of the rock can crack, in what is called "onion skin" weathering.

Weathering Process

The roots of plants growing into rocks also causes weathering, and, to a lesser extent, the action of animals can also weather the rocks. All these methods create rock particles, which are available to mix with organic matter, to form soils.

Organic Matter in Soil

The organic matter is comprised of rotted plants, animal remains, and excreta. Each of these ingredients will also decompose, forming yet more materials. This provides a rick mix of nutrients for the soil, which the next generation of plants will be able to use. There will also be organisms living in this rick mixture, such as bacteria, and a wide variety of invertebrates. During decomposition, many organic compounds are converted into inorganic compounds, such as ions of ammonium, nitrate (V), sulfate (VI), and phosphates.

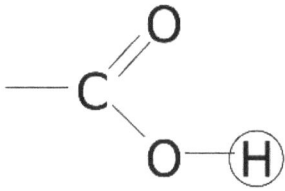

carboxylic acid group   **phenol group**
(ringed H atom is removable, to form negative ion)

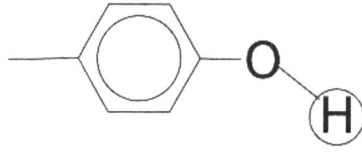

Some of the carbon from decomposition will get into the atmosphere as carbon dioxide. Some of it forms a new range of organic molecules, in a mixture known as humus. Many of these compounds are esters of organic acids. The most common acids will have a carboxylic acid group or a phenol group. The ringed hydrogens in the diagram can ionize, allowing ionic bonds with metal cations to be formed.

Nutrient Cycles

Plants get their nutrients (other than CO_2) from the soil. The various elemental components are cycled between living systems, the organic store (at the top of the soil), and the inorganic store (within the soil). The diagram shows how this happens. The organic store is replenished by animal excretions, organic manure, and death and decay of organisms. Soil microorganisms convert organic matter in humus and inorganic ions. Soil and rock weathering puts ions into the inorganic store. Some nutrients will be lost, by the soil's top layers being leached by rainwater. Nitrates are also lost, by elemental nitrogen gas, and other nitrous gases (NH_3, N_2O), escaping into the atmosphere.

Further Study

Could the concepts mentioned in this section be used to make artificial soil? Find out what hydroponic growth is. How do nutrients reach the plants in hydroponic farming.

What does Organic Mean?

One of the problems in understanding agricultural science is the confusion over the use of the word *organic*. The word is used in three different ways, and you will have to examine the context, in order to determine which one is being used.

1. **Organic material** refers to material in living things, or in dead things that were once alive. In this sense, compost would be comprised or organic material.

2. **Organic chemistry** refers to the study of carbon compounds - except CO2, CO, and carbonates, which are treated as inorganic compounds. In this respect, an organic compound may not have ever been part of a living organism.

3. **Organic farming** refers to farming processes using fertilizers and pesticides of only plant or animal origin. Many states and countries have strict standards, to which farmers must adhere, if their products are to be classified as organic.

Hopefully you can see that these three uses of the word *organic* are not necessarily related.

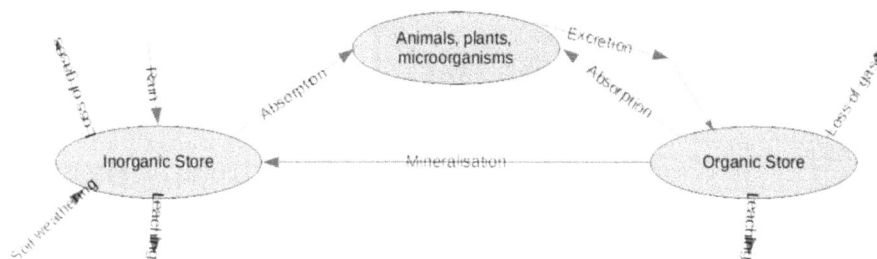

4. Nitrogen and Crops

Nitrogen Fixation

Of the three primary macro-nutrients, possibly the most important is nitrogen. The atmosphere contains 78% nitrogen. However, as an element, it is a relatively unreactive gas, and plants cannot make use of the element. There are a number of processes that can convert nitrogen into soluble ammonium or nitrate (V) ions that plants can use. These processes are called *fixing nitrogen*.

There are certain bacteria that can fix nitrogen. For example, rhizobia bacteria, in nodules on the roots of legume plants, such as peas and beans, can convert nitrogen gas to ammonium ions.

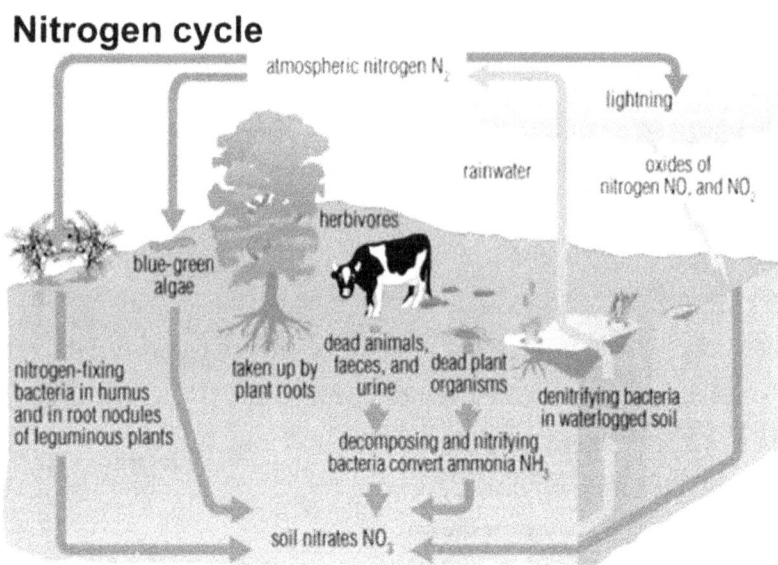

Nitrogen cycle

$$N_2(g) + 8H\cdot(aq) + 6e^- \rightarrow 2NH_4^+(aq)$$

A reducing agent is required, as the source of the electrons.

Additionally, some atmospheric events create some fixed nitrogen. These include lightning, natural fires, and burning hydrocarbon (fossil) fuels, such as in cars. The reaction between nitrogen and oxygen in the atmosphere is endothermic, unlike most oxidations, and the energy input required is provided by the electrical energy of lightning.

$$N_2 + O_2 \rightarrow 2NO$$

Organic nitrogen compounds are broken down by soil bacteria. The resulting ammonium ions can be held by clay. Ammonium ions are oxidized by aerobic bacteria in the soil, to make nitrate (V) and nitrate (III) ions.

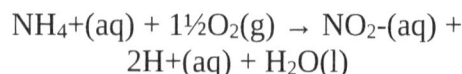

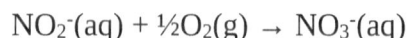

$$NH_4^+(aq) + 1\tfrac{1}{2}O_2(g) \rightarrow NO_2^-(aq) + 2H^+(aq) + H_2O(l)$$

$$NO_2^-(aq) + \tfrac{1}{2}O_2(g) \rightarrow NO_3^-(aq)$$

Assignment

A hectare (ha) is a unit of area, equivalent to a square of 100m. His is equivalent to about 2.47 acres.

Mineralisation has a first-order rate equation:

rate of mineralisation = $k[N]$

where k is the rate constant at a particular temperature and $[N]$ is the quantity of organic nitrogen in the top 20cm of soil.

The rate constant k varies from 0.01 yr^{-1} to 0.06 yr^{-1}. For a time interval of 1 year, the quantity of organic nitrogen mineralised in the top 20cm of soil equals $k[N]$ kg ha^{-1}

Use the equation above to calculate the quantity of nitrogen mineralised in 1 year (in that top 20cm of 1 ha) in the three soils A, B, and C. The soils have different organic nitrogen contents and different temperatures (the value of k depends on the temperature).

Soil	Soil organic N /kg ha⁻¹	Rate constant k /yr
A	1000	0.01
B	2000	0.03
C	2000	0.06

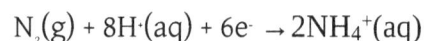

Oats | Beans

Fallow (clover) | Barley

Year 1

Fallow (clover) | Oats

Barley | Beans

Year 2

Barley | Fallow (clover)

Beans | Oats

Year 3

Beans | Barley

Oats | Fallow (clover)

Year 4

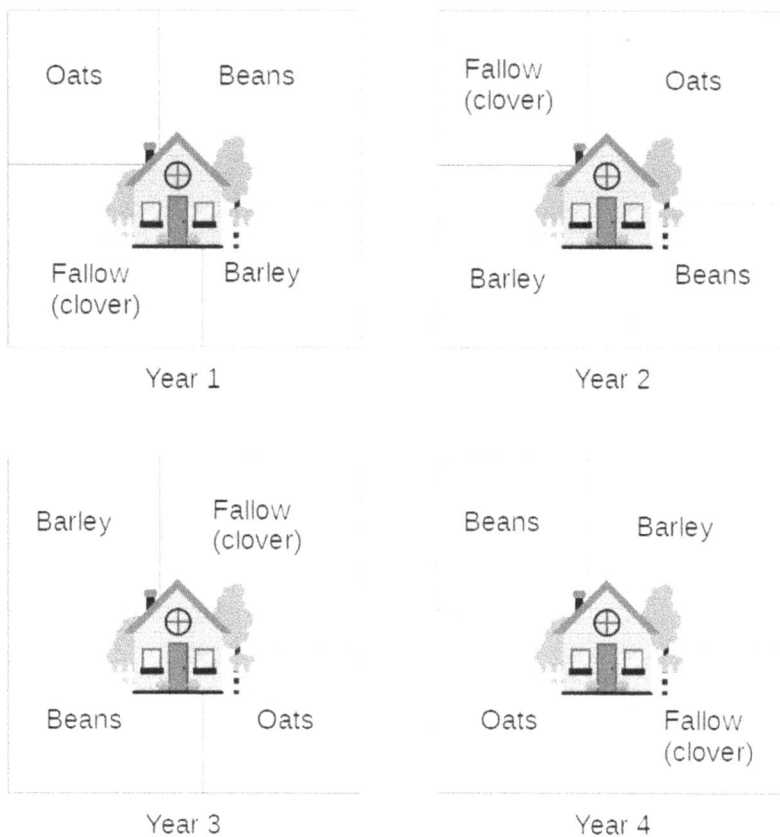

This nitrification can occur in soils down to 0°C (32°F). It cannot occur in waterlogged soils.

Nitrogen Cycle

The various processes that put nitrogen into the soil, or remove it, form a cycle, which is represented in the diagram.

Crop Rotation

Before the science of nitrogen fixation was known, farmers knew to keep their soils fresh, by a process known as **crop rotation**. This was used in medieval England, and its existence is celebrated in a children's nursery rhyme – **Oats and Beans and Barley**. A farm would have four fields. One would be planted with oats, one with beans, and one with barley. The fourth field was left *fallow* – i.e. no crops were grown. However, the most common wild plant to grow in rural England is clover, which is a legume, as are beans. Therefore, two fields were putting nitrates into the soil, while the two cereal crops were removing nitrates. In the second year, the crops planted would be rotated. A four-year cycle of crop rotation kept the four fields in good condition.

Green Manure

A green manure is a crop that is able to fix nitrogen – such as clover or mustard. These crops are usually grown during the winter months, and not harvested. Instead, they are plowed back into the soil, to increase the nitrogen content of the soil. Minerals taken up by these plants are not easily leached from the soil by rain. A crop for harvest can then be planted, to grow through the summer.

Farmyard Manure and Compost

Manure and composted household waste can increase the nitrogen content of soil directly. The use of household compost could be helpful for waste management, as could the use of farmyard manure. Farmyard manure also encourages helpful bacteria and earthworms. However, leaching of manure minerals into water outlets can occur just as easily with farmyard manure as with artificial fertilizers. The table shows the NPK values of two main producers of manure.

	Manure produced /t yr^{-1}	Nutrient content /kg t^{-1}		
		N	P	K
1 dairy cow	23	4.7	0.6	4.4
10 pigs	21	6.3	1.5	2.9

5. Fertilizers and the Haber Process

Nitrogenous Fertilizers

As agriculture became ever more mechanized and industrialized, from about 1700, farmers looked to grow more crops than their villages needed, because there was a growing market for food in the new urban areas. Nitrogenous fertilizers were needed to produce more crops. Two main sources for such fertilizers were resourced in South America. Large amounts of guano – compacted bird droppings – were imported, mostly from Peru. And sodium nitrate was imported from Chile. The latter was also of use in explosives, and it was the need for the latter that encouraged the search for a more efficient source of nitrogen compounds.

Science Museum Group. Diorama of Medieval ploughing, 14th century.. 1944-40. Science Museum Group Collection Online. Accessed September 19, 2019. https://collection.sciencemuseumgroup.org.uk/objects/co38945.

Haber Process for Manufacturing Ammonia

The German chemist, Fritz Haber, developed an industrial process for manufacturing ammonia in 1909. The reaction is slow, and gives a low yield at normal temperatures. The process is still used today, though obviously the system has been tweaked. The reaction requires pure nitrogen and hydrogen. Nitrogen is obtained by the fractional distillation of air, and hydrogen is by the steam reformation of natural gas, which is mostly methane. The equation for the latter is:

$$CH_4 + H_2O \rightarrow CO + 3\,H_2$$

Further hydrogen is obtained by the Water-Shift reaction.

$$CO + H2O \rightarrow CO2 + H2$$

The equation for the Haber Process itself is:

$$N_2 + 3H_2 \rightarrow 2NH_3 \quad \Delta H° = -91.8 \text{ kJ mol}^{-1}$$

The reaction is an equilibrium, involving gaseous molecules, so we can apply Le Chatelier's Principle, in order to maximize the yield.

2.From left to right, 4 volumes (1 of N_2, 3 of H_2) become 2 volumes. Therefore, the forward reaction can be encouraged by increasing the

CC BY-SA 2.0 Generic

pressure on the mixture, so that the reaction attempts to decrease its own pressure to minimize the change.

3.The forward reaction has a negative molar enthalpy – hence it is exothermic, giving out heat. Therefore, a low temperature would increase the yield. However, a low temperature would also adversely affect the rate of reaction. Therefore a compromise temperature is used.

In a typical industrial process, a pressure of 25 MPa (3600 psi) drives the reaction forward and increases the rate. The compromise temperature of about 450°C (840°F) sounds hot, but is actually quite low for an industrial process. Additionally, a catalyst helps to speed up the reaction. Haber used osmium, but this expensive. A cheaper catalyst is made by adding a number of surface impurities to iron.

These conditions give a yield of just 15%. However, ammonia has a much higher boiling point that either nitrogen or hydrogen, so it is easy to remove the product by a little cooling, when the reactants can be recycled and used again.

The ammonia made by this method can be used to make ammonium compounds. Oxidation of ammonia can be used to make nitrates. So a number of compounds used in fertilizers can be made from the product of the Haber Process.

Fritz Haber (1868 – 1934)

• Born in Breslau, Prussia (Germany) (Breslau is now in Poland) in 1868

• Invented the eponymous process in 1909

• 1913 – first industrial plant makes 30 tons of ammonia per day

• Haber also developed chemicals used by Germany in World War I in chemical warfare

• Awarded Nobel Prize for Chemistry in 1918.

• From 1931 onwards, urged his second wife and children to leave Germany for the UK, which they did in 1933. This is because the family was ethnically Jewish, and Haber was concerned by the rise of National Socialism.

Find out more about Haber, to flesh out this brief biography. Also find out about Carl Bosch, the co-developer of the Haber Process (sometimes called the Haber-Bosch Process).

6. Case Study - Pests and Pyrethroids

Pesticides

Crops, being plants, are food not only for humans and domestic animals, but a whole range of destructive bugs. We would define such bugs as pests, because they reduce the crop yield at harvest time. For that reason, an agricultural chemist wants to find pesticide chemicals. Such chemicals need to fulfill a number of criteria.

- They should be specific to the target organism, not killing beneficial organisms
- They should require low doses to kill the target pest, for economical reasons
- They should not persist in the environment after use

Such criteria can be applied to any pesticide chemical. As a case study, we will examine how these strategies were successful in the synthesis of pyrethroid pesticides.

Chrysanthemum cinerariifolium, CC BY-SA 3.0 Unported

Pyrethrin 1

It has been known for centuries that the dried flower heads of a certain species of chrysanthemum can be used to ward off insects. *Chrysanthemum cinerariaefolium* seems particularly good for keeping mosquitoes away. The plant looks similar to a common daisy, and, indeed, all chrysanthemums are part of the *Asteraceae* family, which includes daisies and dandelions. While researching this section, I even found instructions on the internet on how to make your own insecticide spray from the dried flower heads of this plant.[1] The active ingredients were isolated, and their structures determined, between 1920

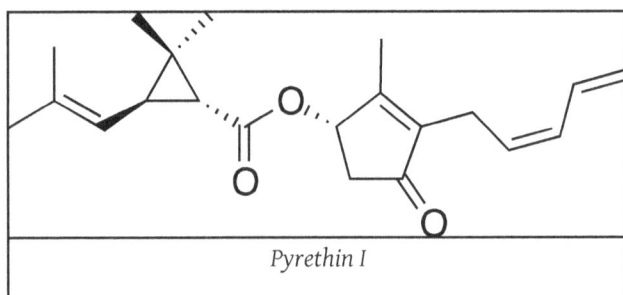

Pyrethin I

and 1955. One of the most important is Pyrethrin I. The structure shown exhibits a considerable amount of stereochemistry, including chirality.

Pyrethroids

The natural pyrethrins from chrysanthemum cinerariaefolium fit the criteria for ideal pesticides. Unfortunately, they are unstable in light, and break down easily and quickly, so cannot easily be used in agriculture. So the search was on to find a related molecule, which could be synthesized, and which would be stable enough to use in agriculture. These synthetic related compounds are known as pyrethroids. The first to be produced was

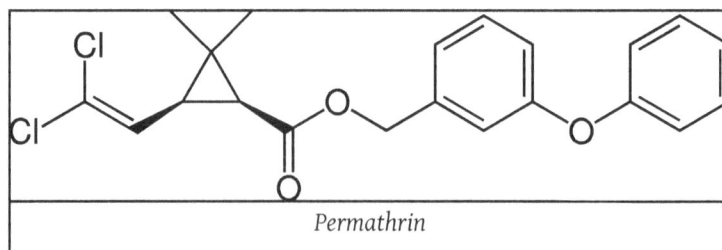

Permathrin

---

[1]   *What Is Pyrethrin Insecticide?*,

< https://www.thespruce.com/pyrethrin-insecticide-definition-1902891 >, accessed 9/20/2019.

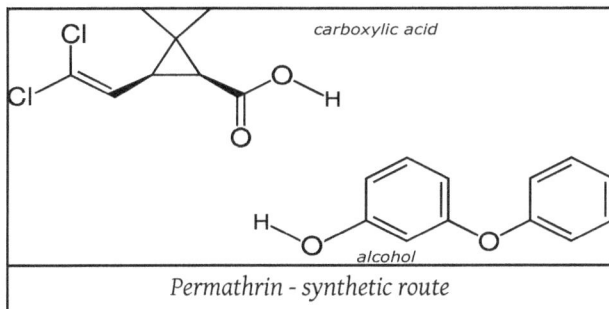

Permathrin - synthetic route

Permethrin, in 1977. Permathrin actually consists of a mixture of four enantiomers, differing only in the arrangement of the groups attached to the cyclopropane ring. The diagram shows the (1S,3S)-cis enantiomer. The synthetic route comprises of several stages. In the diagram, one can see an ester linkage, and this is reacted with a phenyl alcohol, involving the two phenyl rings. Clearly the carboxylic acid with the propane ring must first be prepared, as must the phenyl alcohol.

Biocypermethrin is a similar molecule, with a cyanide group on the ester linkage. Despite the cyanide group, it is still safe for mammals and birds, and is more active at killing insects, so smaller quantities can be used.

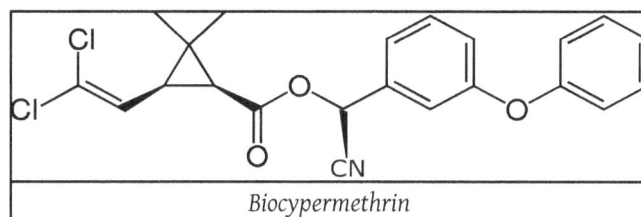

Biocypermethrin

Environmental Considerations

In mammals, pyrethroids are broken down into polar products. These are not attracted to the animal fat, but excreted in urine, as they are water soluble, before they can do any damage. Soil bacteria act similarly on the pyrethroids that are washed from the plants into the soil.

There are, however, issues for humans caused by allergic reactions, or chronic toxicity, through respiration. The natural pyrethrins seem to be more problematic in this regard.

For Further Study

The hydrolysis of biopermethrin in the soil is a first-order reaction. Look this term up. Calculate the half-life of pyrethrin, if there is 2% of the insecticide left in the soil 2 months after application.

DDT

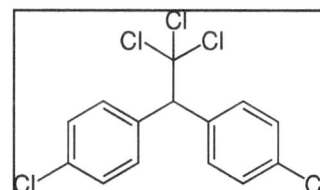

Dichlorodiphenyltrichloroethane, known as DDT, is arguably one of the most controversial chemicals produced in the 20th Century. It was originally developed as an insecticide, and is a colorless, tasteless, almost odorless crystalline solid. It was widely used in the 1940s and 50s to control the insect vectors of various diseases, such as typhus and malaria. In 1955, the World Health Organization initiated a program to eradicate malaria in many parts of the world. This was principally achieved by the extensive use of DDT, to kill disease carrying mosquitos. The program elimated malaria in North America, Europe, the former Soviet Union, much of the Pacific, Australia, and the Caribbean. However, by the early 60s, concerns were being expressed - most notably in Rachel Carson's book, Silent Spring.[1] These concerns eventually led to its being banned in many countries of the world, including the United States.

DDT is a lipiphile. That is to say, it dissolves easily in animal fat, and lipids. Many reports have suggested it is acutely toxic, and even carcinogenic. Other reports - less easy to find on the internet - have commented on the inability of many poorer countries to manage malaria in the absence of the use of DDT.It would be worth your studying reports on both sides of this argument, in order to reach a balanced opinion.

---

[1] Carson, R. (1962, anniversary edn. 2002), *Silent Spring*, (Boston, MA: Houghton Mifflin Company).

7. Herbicides

There will be some occasions when it is necessary to kill of plants, rather than pests. To do this, a herbicide is required. There are two main types of herbicide - **total herbicides** and **selective herbicides**.

Total Herbicides

These are used to destroy all green plant material in the area where a crop is to be planted. It should get the soil completely clean, and reduce the possibility of weeds growing with the crops - preventing tares from growing with the wheat! It is better if the herbicide does not tend to linger in the

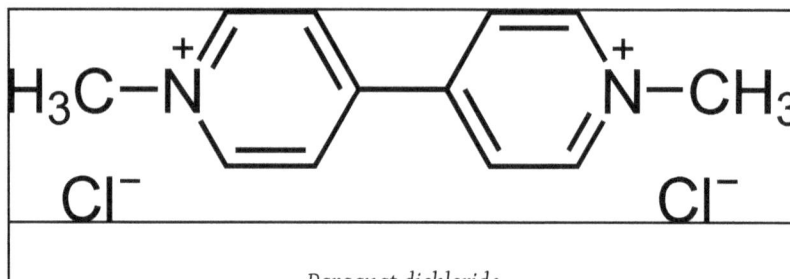

Paraquat dichloride

soil, because if it did so, then a total herbicide could prevent the growth of the new crop.

Paraquat

One particularly well known total herbicide is paraquat. This herbicide is relatively easy to synthesize. Paraquat is formed from pyridine, which is first treated with sodium in ammonia followed by oxidation to give 4,4'-bipyridine. This chemical is then dimethylated with chloromethane to give the final product as the dichloride salt. Other dimethylating agents can be used, giving different salts.

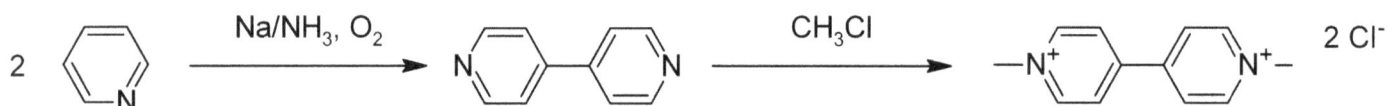

Paraquat was first synthesized in 1882, but was only recognized as a herbicide in 1955. Industrial manufacture of the chemical began in 1962.

Its advantages as a total herbicide are:

- It kills a wide range of annual grasses and broad-leaved weeds and the tips of established perennial weeds.

- It is very fast-acting.

- It is rain-fast within minutes of application.

- It is partially inactivated upon contact with soil.

It is, however, highly toxic to mammals, including humans. For that reason, it has been banned in the European Union. Its use is strictly licensed in the US.

Selective Herbicides

The idea behind a selective herbicide is that it should destroy weeds in crop fields, without destroying the crop plant. A simple poison, like paraquat, will not work for such a scenario. When designing a selective herbicide, a chemist will need to find naturally occurring differences between weed and crop plants, and exploit these difference to kill one without the other. Some herbicides, for example, work most effectively on broad-leafed plants, but not so well on narrow-leafed plants. Cereal crops, being grasses, will usually have narrow leaves. Other selective herbicides might exploit something about the metabolism of the weed plants.

Much research today is focused on genetic modification of plants, to produce strains that are resistant to certain herbicides, so that large scale spraying will kill the weeds, but not the GM crop. However, this leads to fears that the modified gene could jump species into a weed plant, producing "superweeds", which might be resistant to any herbicide.

Organic Pest Control

Organic farming cannot usually use either pesticides or herbicides. Other strategies need to be adopted. A number of strategies can be adopted, to reduce problems. However, none of these strategies will be as fully effective in either pesticidal or herbicidal action, so more crops will be lost. Hence, organic food can often be more expensive that the non-organically farmed alternatives.

We have already mentioned crop rotation, as a strategy for keeping soils nitrated. This can also help reduce pests - particularly those pests that might attack a particular crop, as the crop rotation will not allow that pest to build up in the soil.

Physical barriers can help. Fine netting can prevent cabbage white butterflies from laying eggs on broccoli, for example, thus reducing the loss of the broccoli crop to caterpillars.

Predators can also be introduced. For example, greenfly (aphids) make a tasty snack for ladybugs, so some farmers like to introduce such creatures, who could then reduce the aphid population. Of course, once introduced, there is nothing to stop your ladybugs from flying away to some other field.

Controlling weeds is likely to be possible only by mechanical weeding, which is a hard, back-breaking job. In the UK, there are a small number of herbicides which are allowed to be used, without a farmer losing his or her organic production certificate. An example of such a pesticide would be rotenone.

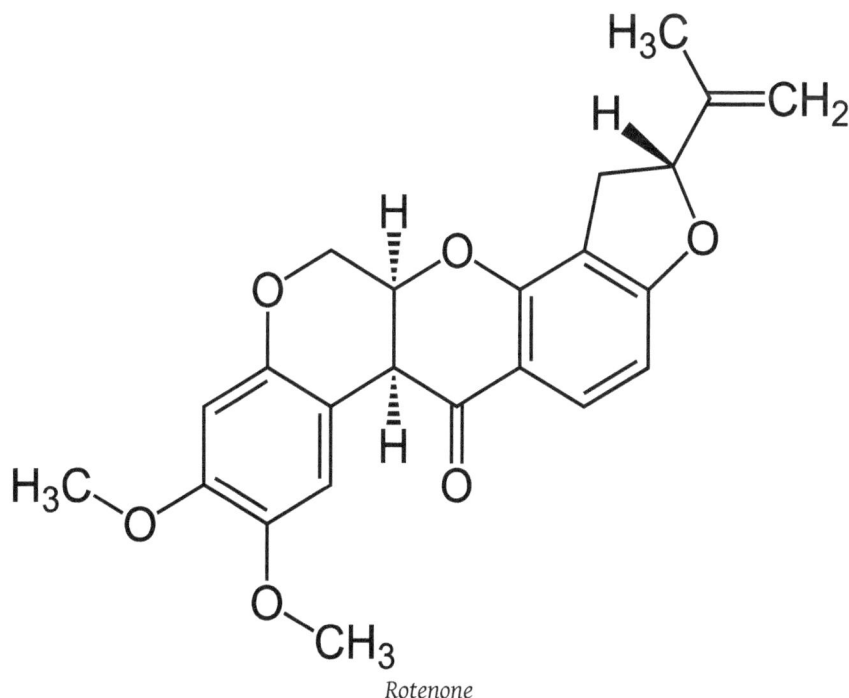

Rotenone

8. Soil pH

Acids and Alkalis in Soil

One of the reasons that the subject of acids and bases or alkalis is such an important subject is its application to a wide variety of real-life situations. The subject is very important as far as agricultural science is concerned. Soils contain varying types of compounds, depending on the rock fragments and organic material found in them. These will contain complex balances of acids, alkalis, bases, and salts. Different food crops require different levels of acidity. Therefore, if a farmer wants to grow a crop that requires one level of pH, in a soil of a different pH, then it will be necessary to adjust that pH, in a manner that will be analogous to the addition of fertilizer. So it will be worth refreshing what you know about these subjects.

Acid

An acid is a molecule capable of donating a proton (i.e. an H· ion). In aqueous solution, the H· ion is, in practice, a $H_3O·$ ion (hydroxonium). Such ionization often happens when the "removable" hydrogen atom is attached to an atom of high electronegativity, such as oxygen (O) or nitrogen (N). Acids in soils will tend to be weak organic acids, rather than strong mineral acids.

Bases

Bases are ionic compounds that will react with acids to form salt and water only. A base is therefore a proton acceptor, accepting the proton donated by the acid.

Alkalis

Alkalis are a subset of bases, being bases that are soluble in water. Soil bases will almost always be alkalis. An alkali in aqueous solution usually has an excess of hydroxide (OH·) ions that can accept protons to become water molecules.

Water and pH

Water is a mostly covalent molecule, though a small number of water molecules dissociate into ions, forming an equal number of H· and OH· ions.

$$H_2O \rightleftharpoons H^+ + OH^-$$

The equilibrium constant by:

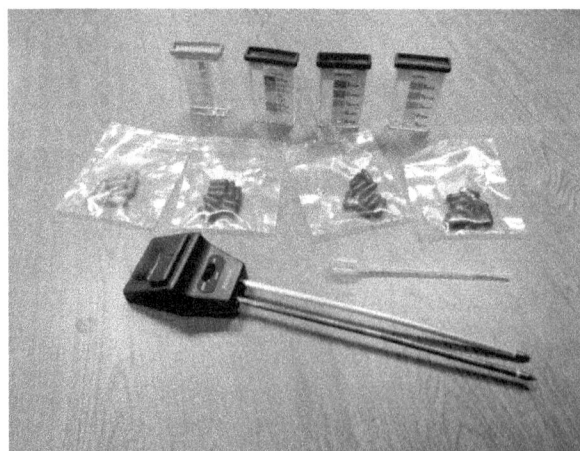

It should be clear that $[H^+] = [OH^-]$. $[H_2O] \approx 1$, and $k = 10^{-14}$.

Therefore, $[H^+]^2 = 10^{-14}$, so $[H^+] = 10^{-7}$.

pH is defined as the decimal logarithm of the reciprocal of the hydrogen ion activity (aH+). The chemical activity is equal to the effective concentration at room temperature and pressure. So, for pure water, pH = 7. If the hydrogen ion concentration is greater than that in water (i.e. acid), then

An example of a soil testing kit and soil pH meter

the pH will be less than 7, while if the hydroxide ion concentration is greater than that in water (i.e. alkali), then the hydrogen ion concentration will be less, giving a pH greater than 7. This definition also shows why a completely dissociated strong alkali will have a maximum pH of 14.

Ion selective electrodes are used to give an electric potential, which can be compared with the potential produced by a standard electrode, with the formula:

$E = E^0 + RT/F \cdot \ln(a_{H+})$

$\Rightarrow E = E^0 - 2.303 \, RT/F \cdot pH$

Hydroxonium Ion - Public Domain

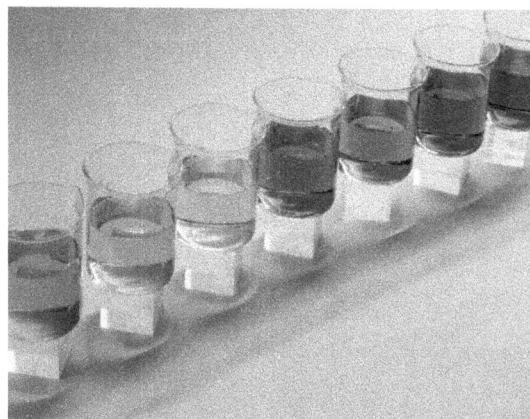

where R is the gas constant, T is the absolute temperature, and F is the Faraday constant. Therefore, pH measurement is temperature dependent, but if every measurement is conducted at the same temperature (25°C), then we can see that the difference between the two electrode potentials is proportional to the pH. So a pH meter is simply measuring potential difference. The meter is first calibrated in a solution of known pH value. There are a number of such solutions that can be purchased (called standard buffer solutions), where the pH is accurately known. When the meter has been calibrated in this way, the scale can easily be adjusted to read the pH.

$$E - E^0 \propto pH$$

Universal Indicator

There are also a number of solutions – mixtures of indicators – which will turn different colors at different ranges of pH values. These indicators can be used in solution, or dried onto paper strips, and will change color at different pH's – the colors being compared with a color chart. This method of measuring pH is nowhere near as accurate as the meter, but is a lot cheaper, and will often give enough information to make decisions on what materials to add to change the soil pH.

The most well-known such solution is marketed as Universal Indicator. A universal indicator is typically composed of water, propan-1-ol, phenolphthalein sodium salt, sodium hydroxide, methyl red, bromothymol blue monosodium salt, and thymol blue monosodium salt. The color red indicates a strong acid, of pH 3 or less. Green indicates neutral (pH 7), while violet is a strong alkali, of pH 11 or more. In between colors are approximately those of the spectrum.

For Further Study

If you can obtain a suitable soil testing kit, like the one shown, try testing at least three different local soils, and write a report of your findings.

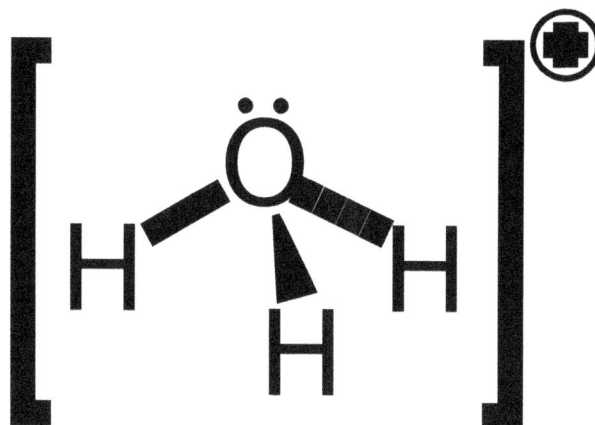

Univeral Indicator, CC BY-SA 4.0 International

9. Greenhouse Gases and the Farm

Methane on the Farm

If you had not noticed that one of the biggest controversies in science today is the issue of Global Warming, or Climate Change, then you must have spent the last few years locked in your attic!

Fresian Cows - Adobe Stock Images

We will explain the issues very briefly here, because we will examine the subject in more detail in a unit about Atmospheric Science. Some scientists are of the opinion that the average temperature of the Earth is getting warmer. This is undoubtedly true – though there have also been periods of time when it has decreased. But modern scientific records began in Victorian times, when the earth was just emerging from the "little ice age", so it would seem obvious that global temperatures would increase. However, many scientists suggest that this warming is caused by human industrial activity – hence it is could more correctly be called Anthropogenic Global Warming (AGW) – warming caused by people. The modern word Climate Change takes into account the fact that temperatures may go down as well as up.

The principle "culprit" chemical, for these opinion formers, is carbon dioxide, which has what is known as a "greenhouse effect", helping to keep solar heat from escaping the earth's atmosphere. This effect is important, because without it the earth would be too cold for life. Some scientists are concerned that industrial emissions of carbon dioxide are causing too much warming, however.

Cow Methane

A close second place, in people's concerns, is taken by methane. This can be released by certain industrial processes, but is also released by a number of agricultural processes. The most well-known of these would be methane caused by cattle. Grass chewed by cows gets fermented, as the cow digests the cud in its multi-stomach system. Under normal aerobic conditions, sugars produced during the digestion of cellulose and starch will oxidize to carbon dioxide and water.

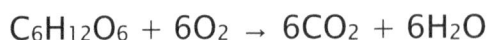

$$C_6H_{12}O_6 + 6O_2 \rightarrow 6CO_2 + 6H_2O$$

If conditions are anaerobic, however, there will be insufficient oxidation, and one of the products created under those conditions is methane. Most of the cows' production of carbon dioxide comes from belches through the mouth, rather than the other end. It has been calculated that a cow might produce more carbon dioxide than the average family car. The question at issue is whether or not this carbon dioxide is really that dangerous.

How Serious is AGW?

This is where we find the real controversy in this subject. The majority of high school textbooks will tell you a great deal about the dangers of AGW, and how seriously we need to control the atmospheric content of carbon dioxide and methane. The intergovernmental panel on climate change (IPCC – ipcc.ch) has produced a number of reports from the climate alarmists' perspectives. To find out some alternative arguments, from the view point of what are known as climate skeptics, I would refer you to websites such as the Cornwall Alliance (cornwallalliance,org), or the Global Warming Policy Foundation (thegwpf.org). The arguments of the latter two organizations cast doubt on the reports of the amounts of methane produced. Also, it has been said that, even if IPCC methods on reducing methane emissions from cows were implemented, the effect on the world at large would be very tiny, compared to the huge increase in food costs, due to lowered availability of meat herds.

For Further Study

By comparing arguments about cattle production of carbon dioxide in the resources mentioned above, write a brief essay, giving both sides of the debate, and your own reasoned opinion.

Other Methane Sources

Other sources of methane include:

• marshes, and landfill sites

• rice paddy fields

• Arctic tundra, when the ice melts

• Partially digested foods

Note

I should remind you again that this section has not been intended to delve deeply into climate change science, but rather just to look at its implications for agricultural science.

CC BY-SA 4.0 International

10. Fish and Chips and Biodiesel

CC BY-SA 3.0 Unported

Brassicas

The word *cultivar refers to different "breeds" of plants, within the same species. For example, domestic dog breeds, such as bulldogs, labradors, and shelties, have been bred for different factors, but are all part of the same dog species. In the plant world, such artificial "breeds" are called cultivars. Carrots and cilantro are cultivars of the same species. One of the most common crop types are the brassicas, especially brassica napus. This latter species includes cultivars such as rutabagas (or swedish turnips or swedes), napa cabbage, bok choy, and rapeseed.

The term rapeseed is widely used in the UK, but not in the US. It comes from a related variety – brassica rapa. Although it is basically the same thing as a rutabaga, rutabaga is grown for a swollen root, whereas rapeseed is grown primarily for flowers, which are allowed to seed, and from which a vegetable oil is produced. This oil is known in the UK as rapeseed oil, but in the US as canola oil.*

Canola Oil

Canola oil is made by slightly heating, and then crushing the seeds. The seeds are cooked to about 88 deg C for 20 minutes. Crushing is achieved by a series of rotating screws. The seeds are squashed into a presscake. More oil is extracted from this by using hexane as a solvent. The solvent can be distilled and re-used. Water precipitation then removes soluble fatty acids and phospholipids. Filtering through clay reduces some of the color, and finally steam distillation removes some unpleasant tasting compounds. Canola oil (or rapeseed oil) is the most common vegetable oil in the UK – in fact, it is usually known as vegetable oil there, whereas in the US "vegetable oil" is usually soya oil.

A higher quality oil can be obtained by cold-pressing, which produces a quality product comparable to virgin olive oil.

Composition

Canola oil mostly consists of esters of fatty acids – as do most vegetable oils. It has a low concentration of

Rapeseed field; CC BY-SA 4.0 International

saturated fats. Most of contents are monosaturated or polysaturated fats, at an approximate 2:1 ratio of mono to poly. Hence, it is thought to be less problematic as far as causing the build up of cholesterol than animal fats. Modern canola oil contains less than 0.01% erucic acid – a compound that caused health concerns in earlier forms of the oil.

Canola Oil 2.0 Generic

Use

At 238°C, its smoke point is high, meaning that canola oil is good for both shallow frying and deep frying. In the UK, it is the most common oil used for deep frying, particularly in fast food shops, such as the famous fish and chip shops.

Another interesting use of canola oil is in the production of biodiesel. This can be used in pretty much the same way as petroleum diesel. However, the cost of producing raw biodiesel is much greater than that of petroleum diesel. Even so, in the US, diesel usually contains about 5% biodiesel.

Biodiesel can be made from used canola oil. In the UK, a large supply of used canola oil is from fish and chip shops. This can be filtered and purified, to produce biodiesel, which, as a product

Mount Washington Cog Railway in New Hampshire uses biodiesel locomotives; CC BY-SA 3.0 Unported

of an otherwise waste material, considerably brings down the cost of the product.

For Further Study

Although as a fuel biodiesel is as effective as petroleum diesel, it does have some deleterious effects on auto engines. Find out what these may be, and how they may be overcome.

This older Mercedes has been converted to run on biodiesel only

11. The Parable of the Sower

To conclude this unit book about agricultural science – Chemistry on the Farm – we will take a look at the Parable of the Sower. This parable, told by Jesus, is found in all three Synoptic Gospels – Matthew 13:1-23, Mark 4:1-20, and Luke 8:4-15. The passages not only relate the parable, but also give Jesus' explanation of why He used parables, followed by Jesus' own exposition of the parable. You would be best advised to read all three accounts, but I will quote just from Matthew.

> And he told them many things in parables, saying: "A sower went out to sow. And as he sowed, some seeds fell along the path, and the birds came and devoured them. Other seeds fell on rocky ground, where they did not have much soil, and immediately they sprang up, since they had no depth of soil, but when the sun rose they were scorched. And since they had no root, they withered away. Other seeds fell among thorns, and the thorns grew up and choked them. Other seeds fell on good soil and produced grain, some a hundredfold, some sixty, some thirty. He who has ears, let him hear." (Matthew 13:3-9)

Jesus does not tell us who the sower is. That is because we can assume it is Jesus Himself, or it refers to the Father, or, perhaps, it refers to us, as we broadcast the Gospel of Jesus Christ. Indeed, it is from this passage that we get the concept of *broadcasting*, which is really an agricultural word; we broadcast the seed.

At no point in Jesus' exposition does He suggest that the sower made a mistake in broadcasting seed into different areas. That is because God knows what He is doing, and the sobering yet glorious truth is that He is glorified, when there are those who reject His word and receive the consequences, as much as when other receive His word and repent.

The first soil is the pathway. The birds represent the devil taking the Gospel message away. That land is open to the elements, and it is easy for the birds to get in and steal the grain. Jesus is reminding His hearers

Pieter Bruegel the Elder, Landscape with the Parable of the Sower

that they should not just ignore His words.

The second soil is the rocky ground. In this case, the plants grow fast, but there is little soil, so they wither away. Jesus says that these people hear the word, and receive it with joy. These are false converts. We should be very skeptical if someone responds to our Gospel message with joy. The normal response to the Gospel is to bring a person to repentance – probably including tears. Joy comes after this. If the joy is immediate, it is likely that they have not really understood the Gospel. If you cannot remember a time when you repented, but only times of "joy in the Lord", please examine yourself, to check whether you have really repented and believed.

The third soil is to do with thorns that choke the word. These are the "cares of the world and the deceitfulness of riches". These plants bear no fruit, and are therefore useless.

Finally, there is good soil. These are people who understand the word; therefore, they will repent and believe. These are those who are genuinely saved, and bear a great deal of fruit.

To do
Pray that God will reveal to you people to share the Gospel with. Pray that their lives will be good soil, and that they will be saved.

Afterword

This unit textbook provides an overview of chemical studies associated with agricultural science.

Further Units

Further chemistry units will address topics such as: *Medicines by Design*, and *Color by Design*.

Mountain Word Science units currently available (September 2019) are:

Chemistry
Oil
Metals
Chemistry on the Farm

Chemistry units in production include:
Color by Design

Physics
Sound and Music

Physics units in production include:
Transporters
The Light Fantastic

If you would like support for any of these units, or any other aspects of physics or chemistry for teenagers, then please do not hesitate to contact us at:

highschool@mshcreationcenter.org

Also, we will gradually be adding support materials on the Mountain Word Academy website at:

https://mwacademy.mshcreationcenter.org

All these materials and textbooks take time and resources to produce. Donations to our ministry can be made at our main website:

https://mshcreationcenter.org

Also, see our publications website:

https://justsixdays.com